T0197588

LUCY
Comes Home

by Debbie Evans

illustrated by Bill McCracken

WestBow Press books may be ordered through booksellers or by contacting:

WestBow Press
A Division of Thomas Nelson & Zondervan
1663 Liberty Drive
Bloomington, IN 47403
www.westbowpress.com
1 (866) 928-1240

Because of the dynamic nature of the Internet, any web addresses or links contained in this book may have changed since publication and may no longer be valid. The views expressed in this work are solely those of the author and do not necessarily reflect the views of the publisher, and the publisher hereby disclaims any responsibility for them.

Any people depicted in stock imagery provided by Thinkstock are models, and such images are being used for illustrative purposes only.
Certain stock imagery © Thinkstock.

ISBN: 978-1-4908-9262-7 (sc)
ISBN: 978-1-4908-9261-0 (e)

Library of Congress Control Number: 2015911159

Print information available on the last page.

WestBow Press rev. date: 08/04/2015

WESTBOW
PRESS®
A DIVISION OF THOMAS NELSON
& ZONDERVAN

Thank you to all of our family and friends who prayed with us for Lucy. A special thanks to my husband who has supported me and prayed for me in this endeavor to complete this work. He has co-labored with me in all things to leave a legacy of faith to our children and grandchildren. Together we pray that this story will echo the faithfulness of God through all generations. This is His story for His glory. It is a true story and a stone of remembrance dedicated to our each of our grandchildren.

"These stones are to be a memorial to the people of Israel forever." —Joshua 4:7

Papa and Mimi had a dog named Lucy. Lucy was a miniature Chihuahua and had everything her little Chihuahua heart could want. Although Lucy was a very little dog, she liked to pretend that she was a big, ferocious dog. "Lucy, go get your bone," Papa said. Lucy ran to her basket of doggie toys as fast as her little Chihuahua legs could carry her, grabbed a bone with her little Chihuahua teeth and took it to Papa. Papa pretended to take it away from Lucy, and Lucy gave a ferocious growl as she and Papa played tug-of-war. Mimi and Papa laughed, and Lucy wagged her little Chihuahua tail with delight.

"... hope in God who richly provides us with everything for our enjoyment." 1 Timothy 6:17

Lucy liked to play like she was a big, brave, ferocious dog, but there was one thing that Lucy was afraid of! Lucy was afraid of storms. She was afraid of the loud thunder when the storm clouds bumped together! She was afraid of the crackling sound of lightning! Lucy would pace the floor with her little Chihuahua legs, and pant with her little Chihuahua tongue, and her whole little Chihuahua body would shake every time it stormed.

"When I am afraid, I put my trust in you; in God whose Word I praise." Psalm 56:3

Today; however, was a beautiful day. The sun was shining and there was a touch of autumn in the air that made Lucy especially excited. "Lucy," said Mimi, "it is time to go outside and play." Lucy jumped down from papa's chair wagging her little Chihuahua tail and headed out the door. Lucy prowled through the big banana trees in her back yard like a lion prowling through the jungle. She barked at the squirrels, chased the cats and basked in the sunshine when she got tired.

"How many are your works, LORD! In wisdom you made them all; the earth is full of your creatures." Psalm 104:24

Lucy was having a wonderful time, when all of the sudden the sky began to grow dark. Rain quickly began to fall, and there was a sudden loud burst of thunder. Lucy was so afraid that she ran to the back corner of her yard to hide from the storm. She discovered a small hole in the fence and made a quick escape. She ran and ran and before long she did not know where she was or how to get back to her safe home! What was she going to do?

Papa and Mimi went to the back door and called Lucy, but Lucy did not come. They looked for her, but they could not find her. Lucy was lost! That night Papa and Mimi were very sad, but they prayed. They asked God to keep Lucy safe and to bring her back home.

"If you remain in me and my words remain in you, ask whatever you wish, and it will be done for you." John 15:7

The next day it was still raining! Papa and Mimi made big signs that said:

LOST CHIHUAHUA - PLEASE CALL 244-4824

They put their signs on telephone poles around their neighborhood and hoped someone would call them if they found Lucy. They looked for Lucy in the rain, but by the end of the day, they still had not found her. That night Papa and Mimi prayed again. They asked God to keep Lucy safe and to bring her back home.

"For the Son of Man came to seek and to save the lost." Luke 19:10

The next day it was still raining, but Lucy's family and friends kept looking for her. They put on their raincoats and rain boots and walked through the woods calling Lucy's name. "Luuucy " they called, but Lucy did not come. That night Papa and Mimi were very, very sad, but they prayed again. They asked God to keep Lucy safe and to bring her back home.

"…He who brings out the starry host one by one and calls forth each of them by name. Because of His great power and mighty strength, not one of them is missing." Isaiah 40:26

After three days had passed, Papa said to Mimi: "I am afraid that Lucy is not strong enough to survive these storms without food or water." Mimi knew Papa was probably right, but she also knew that God was strong, so she kept praying for Lucy. She asked God to keep her safe and to bring her back home.

"…but with God all things are possible." Matthew 19:26

Eight long days passed and finally the phone rang! "Hello" said the voice on the other end of the phone. "I think that I saw a little Chihuahua in my neighborhood - maybe it is your lost dog! Mimi quickly got into her car and drove to the nearby neighborhood. She drove around calling Lucy's name, but Lucy did not come. As Mimi began to drive back home, she decided to drive through the parking lot of a nearby church. She stopped her car, closed her eyes, bowed her head and prayed: "Oh Lord, you see everything." If Lucy is here, please help me to see her also."

"You are the God who sees me." Genesis 16:13

When Mimi opened her eyes, she saw a little dog in the distance running across the parking lot! Could it be Lucy? She called Lucy's name, but the little dog was so tired, and hungry and confused that she began running towards the woods. Mimi quickly got out of her car and walked towards the little dog. "Lucy," she called, "COME TO ME, Lucy!" Lucy perked her little Chihuahua ears straight up in the air. She knew Mimi's voice. She knew she had found her family. Lucy began to run as fast as her little Chihuahua legs could carry her straight into Mimi's arms!

"Come to me, all you who are weary and burdened, and I will give you rest." Matthew 11:28

Mimi picked up Lucy and hurried home to call Papa. Then they called all of their family and friends! Everyone was filled with joy because God answered their prayers. He kept Lucy safe and brought her back home!

"...when he finds it, he joyfully puts it on his shoulders and goes home. Then he calls his friends and neighbors together and says, 'Rejoice with me; I have found my lost sheep'." Luke 15:5-6

"...I ONCE WAS LOST, BUT NOW I'M FOUND"
(from Amazing Grace/John Newton)

Like Lucy was lost from her owners who loved her, because of sin we are lost from God who loves us. Jesus came to rescue us and invites us to come home to Him.

The Bible teaches that God created people to have a relationship with Him.
"I will be their God, and they will be my people." Jeremiah 31:33

The Bible teaches that God is holy – that means He never sins and is separated from all sin and all that is evil.
"Your ways, God, are holy." Psalm 77:13

The Bible teaches that ALL people sin. Sin is disobeying God's commandments and going our own way.
"For all have sinned and fall short of the glory of God." Romans 3:23

The Bible teaches that our sins separate us from God.
"Your iniquities have separated you from your God..." Isaiah 59:2

The Bible teaches that God loves us.
"For God so loved the world that he gave his one and only Son, that whoever believes in him shall not perish but have eternal life." John 3:16

The Bible teaches that God not only loves the world, but God loves YOU – He knows your name and calls you by name.
"...He who brings out the starry host one by one and calls forth each of them by name. Because of his great power and mighty strength, not one of them is missing." Isaiah 40:26

The Bible teaches that Jesus invites us to come to Him for forgiveness. He invites us to rest in everything He has done for us on the cross.
"Come to me all you who are weary and burdened, and I will give you rest." Matthew 11:28

The Bible teaches that when we turn away from sin (repent) to follow and obey Jesus, and place our trust in what He did for us on the cross - that he WILL receive us with open arms.
"...and whoever comes to me, I will never drive away." John 6:37

The Bible teaches that heaven rejoices when we come to Jesus in repentance and faith.
"In the same way, I tell you, there is rejoicing in the presence of the angels of God over one sinner who repents." Luke 15:10

Printed in the United States
by Baker & Taylor Publisher Services